District No. 153

AN EARLY CRAFT BOOK

PAPIER-MÂCHÉ

by BETTY RUMPF   *pictures by* GEORGE OVERLIE

Lerner Publications Company • Minneapolis, Minnesota

LIBRARY OF CONGRESS CATALOGING IN PUBLICATION DATA

Rumpf, Betty.
Papier-mâché.

(An Early Craft Book)
SUMMARY: Instructions for making plaques, tables and chairs, dishes, a pinata, and other objects from old newspapers and paste. Includes suggestions for painting and decorating the finished articles.

1. Papier-mâché—Juvenile literature. [1. Papier-mâché.
2. Handicraft] I. Overlie, George, illus. II. Title.

TT871.R85   745.54   72-13343
ISBN 0-8225-0858-3

Copyright © 1974 by Lerner Publications Company

ISBN No. 0-8225-0858-3

Library of Congress No. 72-13343

Printed in U.S.A.

Contents

A long time ago 5
What is papier-mâché? 7
Papier-mâché plaques 9
Tools and materials 10
A table and chair 18
Bowls and other dishes 23
A piñata 27
Other projects 30

A long time ago

A century ago, when the children in the northern part of the country were celebrating Christmas amid a winter snowfall, the Mexican-American children of the Southwest were celebrating Christmas beneath sunny skies. During their jolly Christmas festival, they had parties every night for two weeks before the holiday. The parties were partly religious pageants and partly pure fun.

Each night during the Christmas festival season, the children and grown-ups in the villages marched in processions, carrying clay statues of Mary and Joseph, the mother and father of Jesus. They marched until they stood in front of a specially chosen neighbor's house. The villagers then chanted prayers and begged to be let in, as Mary and Joseph had done on the night that Jesus was born. The neighbor pretended to refuse at first, but he finally gave in and allowed the other villagers to enter.

The children could barely concentrate on the religious ceremonies that followed because they knew that there was a great treat in store for them. When the chanting and prayers were finished at last, the children began to beg for their treat from the host and hostess. They reminded them that this, more than any other, was a time of special generosity.

But the host and hostess made the children wait just a little longer, until they were very excited indeed. Then, when the time was perfectly ripe for the treat, the host and hostess brought out the long-awaited prize—the piñata. (pin-YAH-tah).

The piñata was a hollow sculptured figure of a donkey, a rooster, or some other favorite animal or toy, and it was brightly decorated with paints and ribbons. The piñata was hung from the ceiling, and, one by one, the children were blindfolded and given a stick with which to hit it. Eventually, one of the children managed to strike home, and the piñata shattered into many pieces. Its splendid contents spilled out onto the floor, and the happy children jostled one another and scrambled to pick up the tiny toys and sweets that had fallen from it.

What is papier-mâché?

The piñata was made of papier-mâché (PAY-pur mash-AY), a versatile modeling material made from shredded newspapers and paste. Because of their piñatas, Mexican-American children were among the first people in this country to learn about making things from this material.

Would you like to learn how to work with papier-mâché? You can make an imitation animal like the children of the Southwest did. You can make sculptures of many different things, and you can make useful things too. You will have lots of messy fun working with papier-mâché.

The words *papier-mâché* are French, and they mean "chewed paper." The words are a good description of what papier-mâché is like,

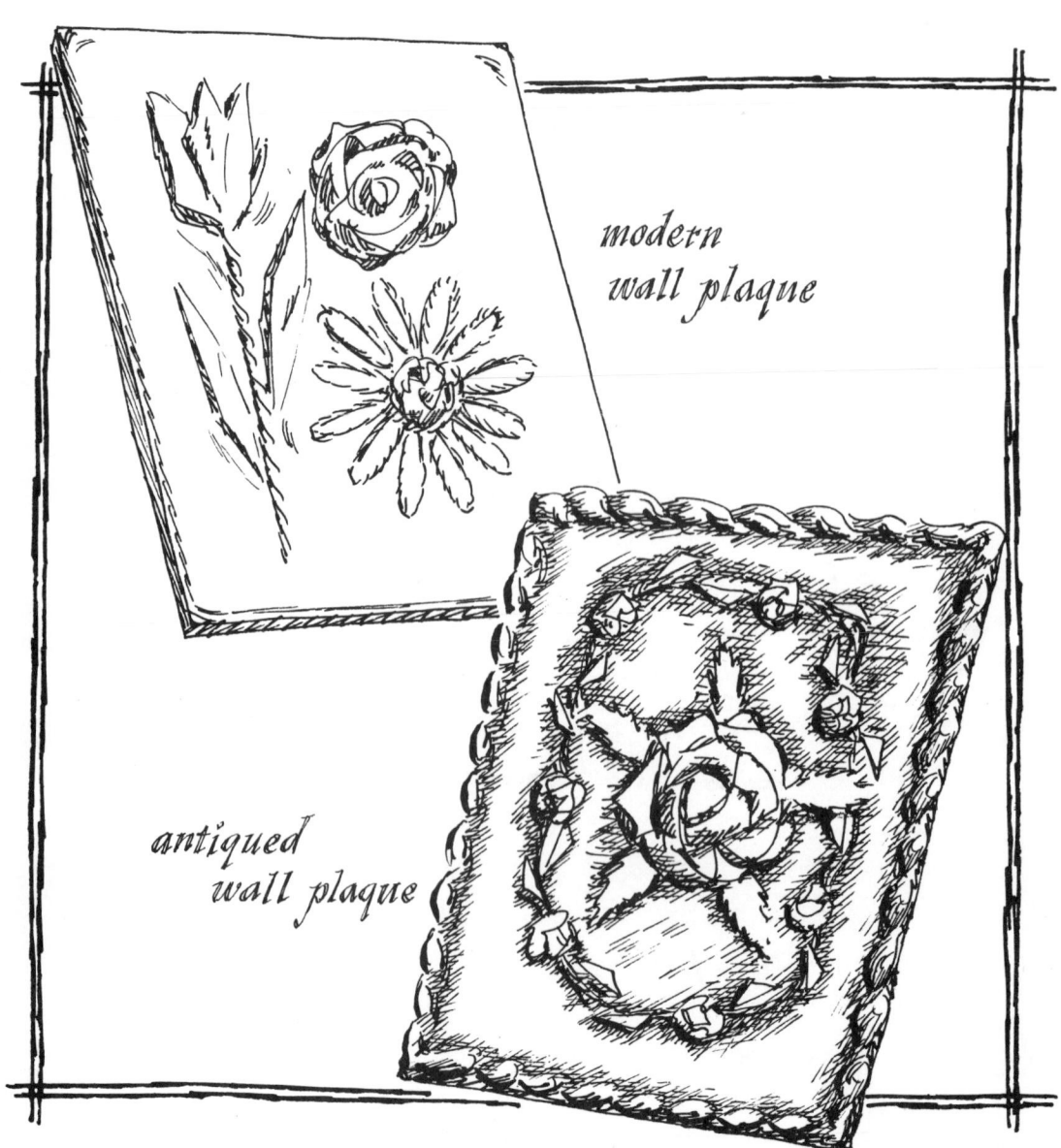

although in English we might describe it as "mashed paper." You probably already have the main ingredients for papier-mâché at home. All you need to start with are flour, water, and newspapers. When you begin to mold and decorate some more complicated things from papier-mâché, you will also need wire, cardboard, masking tape, and paint.

Papier-mâché plaques

Let's begin with a pretty wall plaque. Making it will help you to learn how to use papier-mâché. When you see what you can do with the material, you will be ready to try some molded and sculptured things. You might even want to make a piñata for a party.

You can make a wall plaque that is decorated with a fancy border and with many small flowers in the middle. The plaque will look "antique" if you finish it in a special way. You can also make a wall plaque that is plainer and more modern. You could put just a few flowers on that plaque, or perhaps some circles and triangles.

Tools and materials

However you choose to design the plaque, you will need to gather the basic materials for papier-mâché before you begin. To make the wall plaque, you will need:

> a square or rectangle of sturdy cardboard (Choose a size that is easy for you to handle.)
> 2 cups of flour or dry wallpaper paste (You can buy wallpaper paste at a hardware store.)
> 3 cups of warm water
> a pie pan
> lots of newspapers
> a ball of twine.

cardboard

2 cups of flour or wallpaper paste

3 cups of warm water

ball of twine

pie pan

newspapers

To paint the plaque, you will need:

>a can of gesso (JES-so) (Gesso is a plaster-like substance that looks like whitewash on a finished piece of papier-mâché. You can buy it at a hobby shop.)
>tempera paints in several colors
>liquid laundry starch
>clear plastic varnish
>paint and varnish brushes
>varnish solvent to clean your brushes.

You will also need a clear space to work on. A covered card table makes a good working place. Keep a small basin of water and a towel on the table to clean your hands with as you work.

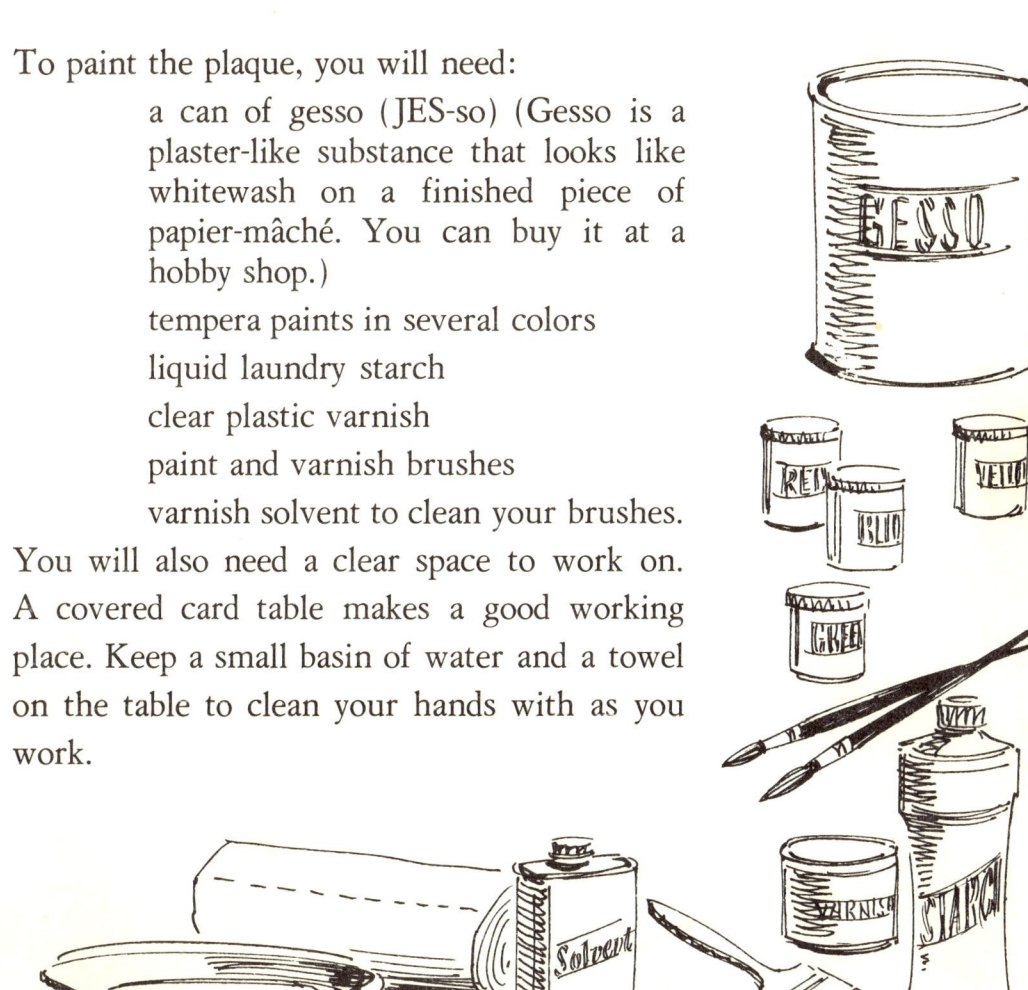

mix flour and water

tear newspaper strips

dip paper in paste

When you have gathered your materials, you may begin to put the wall plaque together. First, you must mix the paste for the papier-mâché. Pour the two cups of flour or wallpaper paste into the pie pan. Then add the three cups of warm water. Mix the flour or paste and water well with your fingers or a stick until all of the lumps are gone. The mixture should look like a gluey soup.

When the paste is mixed, rinse and dry your hands. Then begin to tear the newspapers. Tear several sheets of paper into strips that are two inches wide and longer than the height of the cardboard. Make at least three dozen strips to begin.

Now you can paste the newspaper to the cardboard plaque base. Working with papier-mâché becomes messy fun when you begin to paste. Take a strip of newspaper and dip it into the paste. Cover the strip entirely and remove it from the paste. As you pull the strip out of the paste, clean off the extra paste with your fingers.

Then wind the strip around the cardboard. Wind strips around the cardboard up and down the front of the plaque. All of the newspaper strips should end in the back of the plaque. When you have pasted the strips on up and down the front of the plaque, add another layer of strips going across the front of the plaque in the opposite direction.

After you have pasted all the strips on the plaque, you will see that the cardboard has become stronger and has taken on an interesting texture as well. Fill in the empty space in the back of the plaque with more papier-mâché strips. You can paste in a twine hanger at the same time.

Now you can make some large, splashy flowers. Let's make a big tulip. Take a strip of newspaper about two inches wide and four inches long. Dip it in the paste and clean off the extra paste. Then fold the edges of the paper under and make a point at the top. Attach the tulip petal to the cardboard. Paste on two more

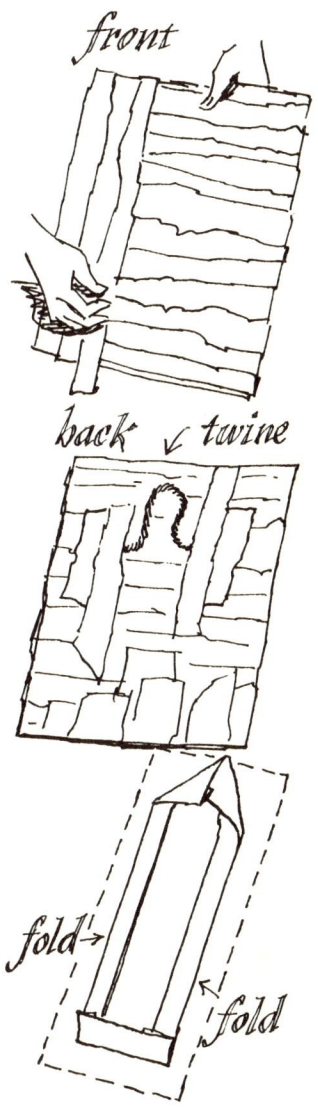

13

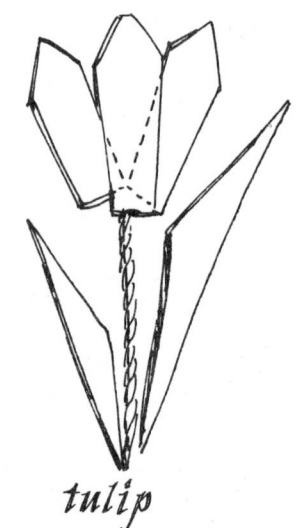

tulip

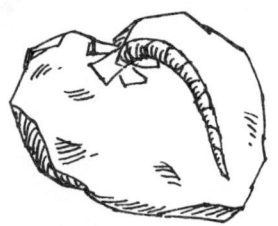

anthurium

petals next to the first. Add a stem made from heavy twine dipped in paste and some long leaves, which can be made in the same way that you made the petals.

Why not try a strange tropical flower next? Tear a piece of newspaper as large as your mother's hand. Dip it in the paste, fold the edges under, and attach the piece to the plaque next to the tulip. Don't smash it down completely. Fasten the edges down, but let part of the flower stand away from the plaque.

Then add a pistil, or center, to the flower. Tear off a three-inch by two-inch strip of newspaper and dip it in the paste. Roll it into a rope. Attach about an inch of one end to the center of the flower. Mold the other end so that it is steady, but so that it stands out from the flower. Did you know that you had made an anthurium (an-THUR-ee-um)?

Let's make one more flower. Let's make a string daisy with a chubby center. Cut a piece of twine that is about a yard long. Dip it into the paste and attach it to the cardboard, forming petals as you lay it down. Let the remainder of the twine extend down from the daisy to form a stem. Add a center to the daisy with a scrunched-up circle of paper, and add long folded strips for leaves.

Your plaque is finished, but it must dry before you can paint it. Let it dry overnight, or put it in the sun to dry. You can also dry it in the oven. Heat the oven to 200° for five minutes. Turn the oven off and put the plaque inside. It will dry there in about an hour.

While you are waiting for the first plaque to dry, you might like to make an "antique" plaque. To begin, paste on strips of newspaper up and down and across on the front of a piece of cardboard as you did for the first plaque. Fill in the back with strips too and paste in a hanger. Now you can add a design. First, put a border around the plaque. Tear off long strips of newspaper that are about three inches wide. Dip one in the paste and lay it down at one edge of the

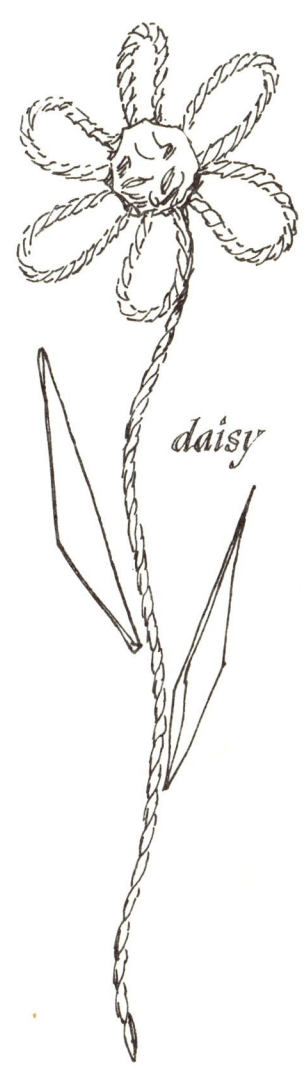

daisy

15

antique plaque

coil – then flatten slightly with hands

plaque. Pinch the paper together at one-inch intervals. It will form a kind of "ruffled" border.

When you have made a border around the entire edge of the plaque, you should plan the design in the middle. Let's make a design using trailing roses with string stems and tiny leaves. You can put a large rose in the center and small trailing roses all around it. The small roses can be connected with string stems and leaves. Mark the plaque with a pencil first so you will know where the roses and leaves should go.

To make the large rose, tear off a strip of paper that is about three inches wide and about twelve inches long. Dip the strip in the paste and then, beginning at the center, coil it onto the plaque. When the strip is coiled, flatten it slightly with your hand. Make smaller roses the same way, but use two-inch by six-inch strips of newspaper. Make leaves from two-inch by three-inch strips. Then paste the string stems on in wavy lines and loops so that the roses look like a trailing bush. Dry this plaque as you dried the first.

16

When the plaques are dry, you may paint them. First, coat each plaque, front and back, with gesso. It will give the plaque a nice white background. Let the gesso dry, and don't forget to clean the gesso brush with warm water and soap.

Now you can mix the paint. Use a paper cup for each color that you need. Mix about two tablespoons of paint with a capful of liquid starch in each cup. The liquid starch will keep the paint from dripping. Paint the plaques in bright, pretty colors. Make a purple tulip, a pink tropical flower, and an orange daisy. Use different shades of red and pink on the antique plaque. Paint the border any color that matches the rest of the plaque.

When the paint is dry, coat both plaques, front and back, with clear plastic varnish. Two or three coats will make the plaques last a long time, and they will also look bright and shiny. Let the varnish dry thoroughly. Clean the varnish brush with solvent as soon as you have finished varnishing. If you don't do this, you

paint on gesso

decorate with paint

varnish

let varnish dry, then rub on antique finish

will ruin your brushes.

If you want your antique plaque to look even older, rub the varnished surface with a bit of cloth that you have dipped in ink or black paint. Remove the excess paint or ink right away, and the plaque will look like it has been darkened with age. Varnish the plaque again to seal the antique surface.

A table and chair

Making plaques will help you to learn how to use papier-mâché. When you have learned the principles of using the material, you can make some more complicated things. Would you like to make a table and chair for your room? You can use the table to hold books or magazines. You can use the chair for a doll seat or as a seat for your favorite hero toy.

To make a table and chair, you will need two very sturdy cardboard boxes. Go to the grocery store and find some boxes that have been used to ship heavy cans or bottles.

Let's begin with the table. Turn one of the boxes upside down. Measure three inches from one of the corners. Using this as a starting point, draw a line from the open end of the box to a point three inches from the surface that will be the top of the table. Then measure three inches from the first line. Draw another line as long as the first line and parallel to it.

cut off end flaps

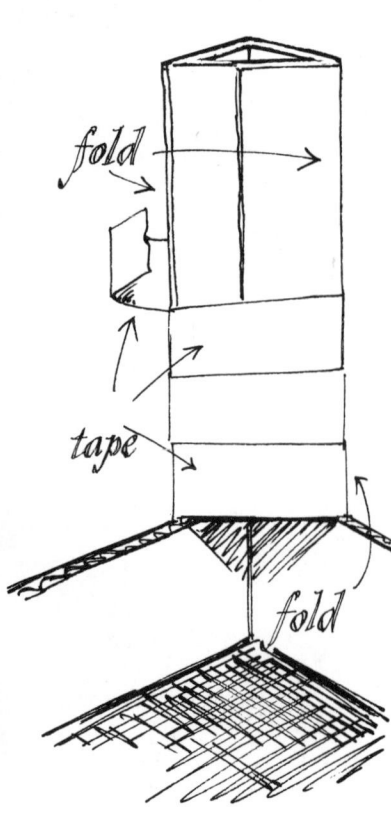

Measure and draw the same set of lines on the other side of the corner. You now have two lines three inches apart on both sides of one corner of the box. Cut on the outside lines at that corner. Then cut the cardboard in to the inside lines. Fold the cardboard on the inside lines.

Repeat the measuring, drawing, cutting, and folding on the sides of each corner of the box. After you have done this, cut the middle flaps of cardboard away. If you tape the folded edges together at each corner, you will see that you have four three-sided legs on your table. Use lots of tape to make sure that the legs are sturdy and are fastened securely.

Then paste two-inch newspaper strips around, across, and up and down all over the table. Be sure to paste them on in layers that go in alternate directions. Paste on at least four layers of strips. Be sure to papier-mâché under the table top too so that the table is completely covered with strips. The more paper you add, the stronger your table will be. Decorate the table with flowers or with other papier-mâché designs made with beans, seeds, ribbon, or rick-rack. Let the table dry as you did with the plaques and then cover it with gesso.

decorate

Now you can make the chair. Make the base of the chair as you did the table, but use a smaller box. Make four strong three-cornered legs. You should also add a back to the chair. Take a strong piece of cardboard that is as wide and as tall as the base of the chair. Cut the cardboard into the shape of a chair back. You can use any one of a number of interesting shapes. You can cut a deep notch in the back. You can cut out a peak. You can cut out rectangular sections so that the chair will look like a ladder-back chair.

Tape the chair back firmly onto the chair base. Then cover the entire chair with strips of pasted-on newspaper. Cover it with at least four layers of strips that are pasted on in alternate directions. Make the joining of the back to the seat very strong and firm.

You might like to use beans to decorate the chair. If you use beans, you can put them on with glue after the chair dries. Put a border of beans around the edges of the back. Make a flower, or a sailboat, or a sun face, or a bird in the center. When the chair is dry and you cover it with gesso, cover the beans too so that the paint will stick to them. Then paint the chair and the table. Paint the beans in bright colors, and then varnish both the chair and table thoroughly and let them dry. You may antique the furniture if you like and give it another one or two coats of varnish. Put the table and chair in an empty corner and let them brighten up your room!

Bowls and other dishes

You really ought to have some dishes to put on your table. You can make a small set of "china," or you can make some unusual "rock bowls." Let's try the rock bowls first. They are quite easy to make.

Finding the rocks from which you will make the bowls is an interesting project in itself. Look on the beach, in the woods, or in your yard. Find some nice bumpy rocks in different sizes. You can make papier-mâché bowls from all of them, but you might like to try a nice fist-sized bowl to start with.

grease rock

apply dry paper strips —
— then apply paste covered strips

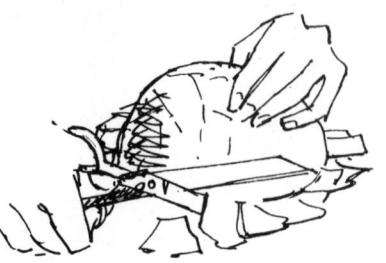
remove when dry — then trim

First, grease the rock well with Vaseline. Then lay a layer of *dry* paper strips over the Vaseline, but leave the top one-third of the rock uncovered. The dry strips and the Vaseline will make it easier for you to remove the finished bowl. When the dry strips are laid down, you may begin to lay on strips of newspapers that have been dipped in paste. Put strips of paste-covered paper over the bottom two-thirds of the rock until you have built up about eight or nine layers. Remember to paste the layers on in alternate directions and to keep the bottom of the bowl flat so that it can stand up.

Let the papier-mâché dry over the rock mold thoroughly. When it is dry, remove the bowl from the rock and trim the rough edges from the top with a scissors. You might want to papier-mâché the rim of the bowl once more to make it smoother. After the bowl has dried again, you may gesso it and paint it as you like. You might like a bold Indian design on some of your rock bowls.

You can make cups, plates, and spoons with papier-mâché in the same way that you made

24

the rock bowls. To make a cup, cover the underside of a small china bowl with Vaseline. Lay dry paper strips on it, and then cover the bowl with papier-mâché strips. To make a handle for the cup, wrap four strips of papier-mâché around a piece of sturdy wire. Then bend the wire and push the ends of it into the soft papier-mâché on the bowl. Because the cup will be very lightweight, the paper handle will support it quite well. Paste strips over the joining of the handle and let the cup dry. When it is dry, remove the papier-mâché cup from the mold and trim the edges.

Make papier-mâché plates from a small salad plate, and make a papier-mâché spoon from a kitchen spoon. Before the plates have dried, decorate them with beans and seeds. Then, after they have dried thoroughly, cover them with gesso, paint the seed designs, and glaze all of the dishes with several coats of varnish. You can eat from these dishes and wash them, just like china dishes. If you have varnished carefully, the papier-mâché will not dissolve in water.

A piñata

Now that you have made plaques, furniture, and dishes from papier-mâché, perhaps you might like to make a gay piñata for a special occasion. Let's make a pretty donkey, with a long, fluttery mane and tail. You can fill his middle with toys, beads, and many different kinds of candy.

A blown-up balloon would make a good mold for the donkey piñata. Blow up a large egg-shaped balloon. Then tear up about three dozen three-inch by four-inch strips of newspaper. Paste a layer of strips all over the balloon, and make sure that they are all pasted on in the same direction. Then paste another layer going in the opposite direction over the first layer. Paste on at least four layers of papier-mâché strips.

Let the papier-mâché dry, and then puncture the balloon at one end with a pin. If you listen carefully, you can hear the air hiss as it goes out of the balloon. Now you should make a hole in

cut end off stuff with treats

~ seal hole ~

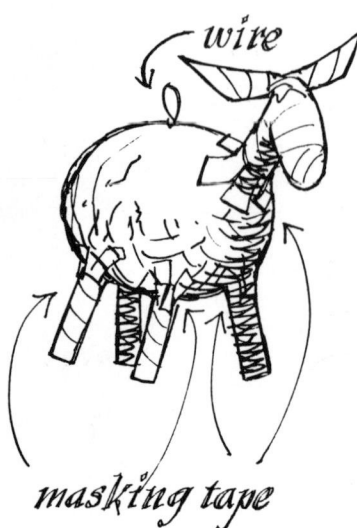

wire

masking tape

the molded papier-mâché. Use a bread knife with a serrated blade and saw about a one-inch section off the end of the papier-mâché ball. Stuff the ball with treats.

When the ball is stuffed full, you may begin to put the rest of the piñata together. Put tape and papier-mâché strips over the hole to seal the treats inside. Then use lengths of paper-towel rolls to make four legs and a base for a head. Attach the rolls firmly with masking tape. Paste layers of newspaper strips over the legs, and build up the head, nose, and ears with many layers of papier-mâché. To make a hanger for the piñata, attach a thin bent wire to the top with tape and papier-mâché.

When your donkey piñata is plump and sturdy, you can add the streamers that will form his mane and tail. Use colored crepe paper for this part of the piñata. Cut the crepe paper into streamers that are about two feet long. Dip one end of each streamer into the paste and then fasten that end to the donkey's neck. When he has a nice flowing mane, attach crepe paper strips to his behind to make a pretty tail.

Let the piñata dry thoroughly, and then cover it with gesso as you have done before. You can paint the donkey a "donkey" color like light brown or soft gray, or you can paint him with bright, surprising designs and colors. Be careful so that the mane and tail do not get damaged or pulled off when you decorate the piñata. You can tie them together to keep them out of the way.

Make some other piñatas. Try an airplane, or an elf, or a fat cat. They are beautiful to look at, and they will help make all of your parties and get-togethers more exciting. A piñata would make a very nice birthday gift too.

tie mane and tail decorate

Other projects

You can also make funny heads and animals with balloons and papier-mâché. You can make a pretty doll's face, or you can make a funny clown face. You can add a beak, some wings, and flat feet to a papier-mâché ball to make a dressed-up penguin. If you put a papier-mâché head on a papier-mâché base, you can use the head to hold your hat or a wig.

You can make some hand puppets and a stage from papier-mâché. Make a puppet head from a small papier-mâché-covered balloon. When the balloon is covered with papier-mâché, make a whole in the bottom and insert a two-inch length of paper towel roll for the puppet's neck. To make the puppet's body, sew a sack dress that has two "arms" and two open ends. Sew the arm holes together at each end. Attach one open end of the sack to the neck firmly with staples or glue. When you make the puppet act, you can put one finger in each arm and another in the head to make it move.

papier-mâché head

puppet dress

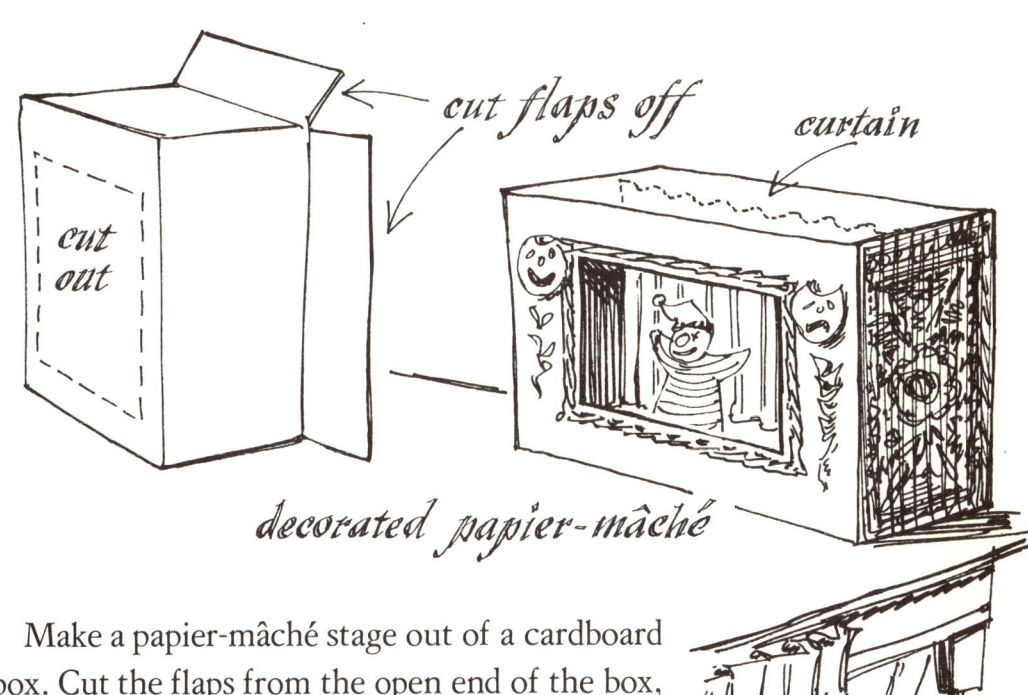

Make a papier-mâché stage out of a cardboard box. Cut the flaps from the open end of the box, and then cut a large hole at the top of the box on the opposite side. Cover the entire stage with papier-mâché strips and decorate the front with papier-mâché scrollwork and flowers. If you hang a curtain from the middle of the box, your wrists will be hidden from your audience when you make your puppet act.

Now you can make many different things from papier-mâché. You can learn how to make

more complicated things just as easily. All you need to do is to figure out how to make a skeleton, or "armature" (ARM-ma-choor), for the things you mold and model. A search of the house will provide some answers. If you want to make a figure with legs and arms, you can tape paper rolls or cups onto a papier-mâché balloon or a plastic bottle. Build the figure around the skeleton with strips of papier-mâché as you did with the piñata. You can also use cardboard for many kinds of figures. Pliable wire makes an excellent armature. You can buy it at a hardware store, and it is not very expensive.

None of the materials that go into a papier-mâché article are expensive. In fact, people who work with papier-mâché perform a service with their craft. They recycle, or reuse, paper, and they reuse it in a way that makes our lives more beautiful and satisfying. Have fun making things from papier-mâché! It is a very free and easy kind of craft.